LEBANON

GROLIER
EDUCATIONAL

Published 1999 by Grolier Educational
Sherman Turnpike, Danbury, Connecticut.
Copyright © 1999 Times Editions Pte Ltd, Singapore.

CIP information available from the Library of Congress or the publisher

Set ISBN: 0-7172-9324-6
Volume ISBN: 0-7172-9333-5

Brown Partworks Ltd.

Series Editor: Tessa Paul
Series Designer: Joyce Mason
Crafts devised and created by Susan Moxley
Music arrangements by Harry Boteler
Photographs by Bruce Mackie
Subeditor: Roz Fischel
Production: Alex Mackenzie
Stylists: Joyce Mason and Tessa Paul

For this volume:
Writer: Richard Kennedy Walker
Editorial Assistants: Hannah Beardon and Paul Thompson

Printed in Italy

Adult supervision advised for all crafts and recipes, particularly those involving sharp instruments and heat.

CONTENTS

LEBANON:

Lebanon is smaller than the state of Connecticut. It borders the Mediterranean Sea in the west. It shares its northern and eastern borders with Syria, and has a short southern border with Israel.

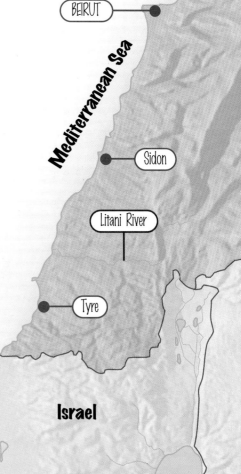

BEIRUT

Mediterranean Sea

Sidon

Litani River

Tyre

Israel

▶**The remains of ancient** civilizations are dotted across Lebanon. Humans have lived along these shores for thousands of years, and the names of many cities can be found in the Bible. The Ancient Egyptians, Persians, and Greeks left their mark. The Romans ruled this part of the world from 64 B.C. until the end of the fourth century. These Roman ruins can be seen in the fertile farming area of the Bekaa Valley.

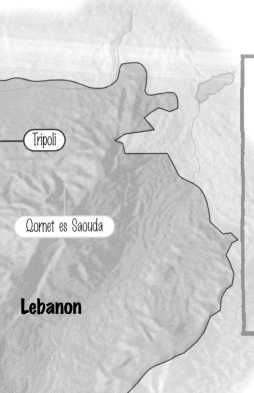

Tripoli

Qornet es Saouda

Lebanon

Syria

First Impressions

- **Population** 2,915,000
- **Largest city** Beirut with a population of 1,500,000
- **Longest river** Litani
- **Highest mountain** Qornet es Saouda at 10,128 ft.
- **Exports** Fruit, vegetables, eggs, chemicals
- **Capital city** Beirut
- **Political status** Republic
- **Climate** Varies according to altitude. Generally hot and sunny.
- **Art and culture** Many ruins from Ancient Greek, Roman, and Phoenician civilizations. Famous writer Khalil Gibran. Famous singer Fairouz.

▶**The Taynal Mosque**
in Tripoli is a fine example of Muslim architecture. It was built in 1336 and was constructed over the remains of a Christian church. The building expresses the mixture of religions found in this country. There are 17 religious groups, broadly split between Muslim and Christian sects.

◀**Beirut was famous** for its beauty. Built on the shores of the Mediterranean, it was both a holiday resort and a successful banking city. However, the civil war that raged in the country from 1971 until 1992 destroyed the city. The Lebanese are determined to regain the former elegance of the city. They are rebuild-ing it so that it resembles the city they lost. This is an artist's impression of how the new Beirut will look.

RELIGIONS

Everybody in Lebanon prays to the same God, but they do so in many different ways. That is one reason why they have many festivals.

MOST LEBANESE are Muslims, who believe God spoke to people through Mohammed, their prophet, or holy teacher. Many others are Christians, who believe God sent his own Son, Jesus Christ, down to Earth to instruct people how to behave. Jesus lived all his life in a place very near to Lebanon, and so many of the Lebanese people became Christians in very early times.

There are many kinds of Christians. The largest Christian group in Lebanon is known as the Maronites. They are named after Saint Maron, a holy hermit who lived in a cave on a river-bank 1,600 years ago. The Maronites pray in a very old language, similar to the one that Jesus spoke. They are recognized by the pope in Rome as a branch of the Roman Catholic Church.

There were no Muslims in Saint Maron's day. Mohammed was not born until 200 years later, hundreds of miles away across the Arabian desert. When Mohammed received messages that were said to come from God, the Arab people rushed from the desert to spread the news. In a very few years the Arabs conquered many lands whose peoples became followers of Islam. This is an Arabic word meaning "to surrender to the will of God."

Muslims, like the Christians, soon divided into groups. The major division is between Sunni and Shi'ah Muslims, who could never agree on who should be in charge. Sunnis make up the majority in most Muslim lands, but not in Lebanon. Here the Shi'ahs are the largest of all the religious groups.

GREETINGS FROM **LEBANON!**

The Lebanese are proud of their descent from the Phoenicians, seafarers whose trading ships reached as far as Britain in ancient times. They are traders still, and great travelers. Lebanese communities are dotted around the world. Their language is Arabic, but when chatting among themselves, they are quite likely to break into French or English, sometimes using all three languages at the same time! Their capital, Beirut, used to be called "the Paris of the Middle East," but it has been badly damaged by war and invasion.

How do you say...

Hello

Marhaba

How are you?

Kifak?

My name is ...

Ismeh ...

Goodbye

Ma'a salama

Thank you

Shukram

Peace

Salam

RAS ISSINI

This festival celebrates the New Year in Lebanon. It is a huge event, and even though the weather is damp and cold, everyone is happy and joyful.

Ras *Issini* means "Head of the Year," and is the Arabic term for New Year in Lebanon.

On December 31, New Year's Eve, families in Lebanon gather at the home of their most senior member. The house has to be quite big, so all the guests can fit in.

Old and valuable handcrafted possessions are the pride of every Lebanese family. They are displayed at celebrations and are passed down to the children when they grow up.

During this party, the family joins hands for the national dance, the *dabki*. They dance to the tune of the *nay*, a kind of flute, and the beat of the *dirbakeh*, a drum shaped like a flower vase. Children clap hands in time. At midnight, church bells ring out, and men shoot guns into the air.

AR-ROUZANA

Ar-Rouzana, Ar-Rouzana,
She is my paradise,
She is the only girl for me,
You must so agree.

The next day, New Year's Day, people get up very early and exchange the cheerful greeting *Kul 'aam u antum salimoun* – which means "Good health be with you each year."

New Year is shared with relatives. Tables are laden with festive food, and folk music and dancing are an essential part of the fun. This fiesta is a happy family day.

AR-ROUZANA

Ar - rou - za - na, ar - rou - za - na, Koul - lee ———— ha - na fi - ha, Shou 'im li - tir rou - za - na, Al la - - i — ja - zi - ha.

MAKE WORRY BEADS

All over the eastern Mediterranean men can be seen carrying "worry beads." These beads have a religious value for Muslims.

YOU WILL NEED
All-purpose glue
Knitting needle
Lengths of colored thread
Small square of cardboard

In Lebanon these beads are called *masbaha*. There is another Arabic word for them, which is *tasbih*. This word means "glorification." The beads are similar to the Christian rosary in that the beads help to keep count of the number of prayers being recited. However, the beads are not always used for prayer, but may be simply held in the hand to bring a sense of tranquility to the person carrying them.

1 Cut triangles 1" at widest base. Make them 23" long and cut to point at apex.

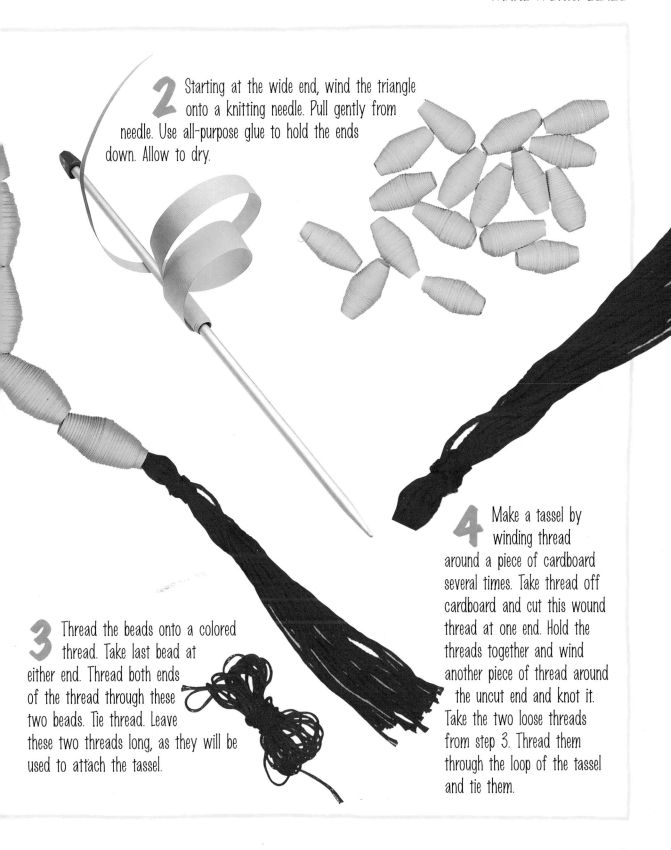

2 Starting at the wide end, wind the triangle onto a knitting needle. Pull gently from needle. Use all-purpose glue to hold the ends down. Allow to dry.

4 Make a tassel by winding thread around a piece of cardboard several times. Take thread off cardboard and cut this wound thread at one end. Hold the threads together and wind another piece of thread around the uncut end and knot it. Take the two loose threads from step 3. Thread them through the loop of the tassel and tie them.

3 Thread the beads onto a colored thread. Take last bead at either end. Thread both ends of the thread through these two beads. Tie thread. Leave these two threads long, as they will be used to attach the tassel.

EID IL FASIH

Eid *means "festival," and* **Eid Il Fasih** *is the festival of Easter. After 40 days of fasting Lebanese Christians celebrate the resurrection of Jesus Christ in April.*

Easter is an important and joyful celebration that marks the day Jesus rose from the dead. It is celebrated throughout Easter week in April and ends Easter Monday. All Lebanese Christians fast the 40 days up to Easter during *Es Soum,* or Lent, to mark the time Jesus spent fasting in the desert. During this period devout families do not eat meat.

Sha'aneeni, or Palm Sunday, the Sunday just before Easter, is a special time for Christian children. They are dressed in their very best clothes for the *Ziah,* a parade around the church just before midday. The smallest children are carried on their parents' shoulders.

The children carry candles, some as tall as themselves, that are decorated with flowers and olive branches. As usual with a Lebanese festival, the day ends with a feast.

The rest of the Easter week passes quietly. Families go to church and eat simple food, but once Good Friday

Candies are a great treat at Eid Il Fasih. Special favorites are the round ma'amoul cookies stuffed with walnuts or pistachios, and also square chunks of raha, or Turkish delight, flavored with rose water. The Easter eggs below get their color by being boiled with red onion skin.

TABOULEH

Place the bulgur wheat in cold water in a bowl and soak for 15 minutes. Rinse, then squeeze dry. Put the bulgur wheat into a large bowl. Add the lemon juice, salt, and pepper, and stir. Leave for a few minutes while you chop the scallions, parsley, and tomato.

Add the oil and stir. Add the scallions, parsley, tomato, and mint. Stir.

Serve cold as a first course or side salad.

SERVES FOUR

⅔ cup bulgur wheat
2 lemons, juice only
salt and pepper
6 scallions
10 oz flat leaf parsley,
2 T. dried mint
1 tomato
5 T. olive oil

has passed, everyone begins to get excited. On Saturday all the churches are lit with candles. The day is called *Sabt innour*, the "Sabbath of Light," because it is said that many years ago lights appeared by miracle in churches throughout Lebanon.

On *Eid likbeer*, or Easter Sunday, everyone puts on their best clothes and goes out to enjoy the warm spring weather. All the children hunt for brightly colored Easter eggs and then knock them together in a game called *youdakis*.

Everyone then sits down to a traditional Easter meal. They eat *kousa*, or zucchini, and grape leaves stuffed with rice and meat, and *Tabbouleh*, a salad with bulgur wheat.

Ithnayn il Rahib, Easter Monday, is the end of the long Easter vacation. Families take trips into the country, and people often let off loud fireworks.

During Es Soum some families may do without olive oil in their food, which is a great sacrifice because they use it so much.

13

EID ISSALEEB

This festival, on Saint Helena's Day, celebrates the ancient tale of the discovery of the most sacred object of the Christian faith – the actual cross on which Jesus was crucified.

Eid Issaleeb, which is the Festival of the Sign of the Cross, is celebrated on September 14, Saint Helena's Day. On that night hundreds of bonfires are lit across the country, while the church bells ring out. The fires flicker across the mountains, and they can be seen from far away, even at sea. They look very pretty.

The fires are part of a very old story that says a saintly queen named Helena discovered the wooden cross on which Jesus was crucified. The queen was so delighted that she ordered a chain of fires to be lit right around the coasts of the Mediterranean Sea to signal the good news to people in other lands.

Children spend all summer gathering dry branches, twigs, and pine needles. This kindling is added to the wood that will be set alight in every Christian village, in churchyards, in fields, and even on the flat roofs of houses on the night of *Eid Issaleeb*. Candles are lit, and lots of fireworks are let off, adding to the excitement.

After all this work the hungry villagers often eat *kibbeh*, a minced lamb a little like a hamburger.

The weather gets cold in September. As the festival of Eid Issaleeb gets closer, people all over the

country look closely at the skies for the first sign of rain. Even if a tiny amount falls on the night before Eid Issaleeb, it is considered a blessed event.

If it does not rain, Lebanese people also believe that water heated over an *Eid* bonfire is blessed with great healing powers. Many people save the water and bathe their eyes in it.

All the Christian villages have at least one patron saint's day. Some villages have two or three saints' days. One group, the Maronite Christians,

who came from nearby Syria ages ago, have a patron saint, too, called Maron.

Saint Maron lived just after Saint Helena. He wore goat skins and prayed standing up all night. When the word spread round that his prayers were able to cure the sick, many pilgrims came to his cave, and he became famous.

As well as growing juicy oranges, Lebanese farmers harvest the orange blossom to make into an essence for flavoring food and lemonade. An essence holder is on the opposite page.

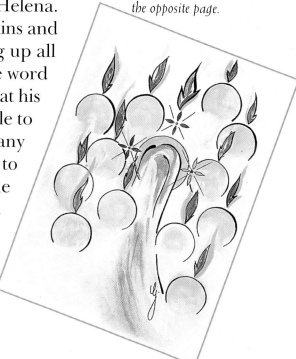

As the mountains flicker with festive flames at the Festival of the Sign of the Cross, farmers are preparing to harvest the ripe grapes grown all over Lebanon's mountains, along with figs, pears, peaches, and apples.

THE STORY OF SAINT HELENA

It is claimed that Saint Helena found the true cross upon which Jesus died. Different Christian countries tell their own version of her miraculous discovery. This is a story told in Lebanon.

QUEEN HELENA was a humble innkeeper's daughter who became the mother of Constantine the Great, the emperor who made Christianity the religion of the ancient Roman world.

The emperor became a Christian after a blazing cross appeared to him in the sky, just before he fought and won his most important battle. His devout mother, Helena, soon began to wonder what had become of the actual cross on which Jesus was crucified in Jerusalem 300 years before.

Helena lived far from Jerusalem in the city of Constantinople, now called Istanbul, in Turkey. In the year 325 at the great age of 72 she set out for Jerusalem. After a long search she found three buried crosses and had them dug up. Helena now had a new problem. How could she know which was the cross on which Jesus Christ had been crucified?

Helena prayed, then she asked the advice of a wise man, who told her to have a dying woman laid on each cross in turn. When the woman was laid on the true cross, she immediately jumped up, strong and healthy again.

Helena died not long afterward and was made a saint. No one knows what happened to the cross, although

it is said that pieces of it were sent to Constantinople and Rome.

The cross is part of many fabulous legends. According to one, it came from the bough of a tree from the Garden of Eden. When Adam and Eve were driven out of the garden, they took the bough with them, and it was used as a beam in Noah's Ark, then as part of King Solomon's Temple, before finally being used to form the cross.

More amazing tales were told of Saint Helena herself. People in Britain once believed that she was the daughter of Old King Cole, the legendary king of the nursery rhyme. This is why several places in Britain are named Saint Helens.

EID AL-FITR

Muslims celebrate the end of the holy month of Ramadan with gifts, greetings cards, family feasts, and visits to friends. It is a little like Thanksgiving and Christmas rolled into one.

Eid *Al-Fitr* means the "Festival of Fast-Breaking."

It celebrates the end of Ramadan, a holy month of fasting in the ninth month of the Muslim calender.

During Ramadan nobody is allowed to eat or drink anything from sunrise until sunset. Only the very old, the very young, and the sick are excused. After sunset everybody sits down to the *iftar*, a big, delicious meal.

As the month of Ramadan comes to an end, everybody gets very excited. Each family gives a little of its money to the poor in a donation called the *zakat*, and pretty greetings cards are posted to friends. On the last night the people stay up late

Children put on their nicest clothes, and mothers wear their best jewelry for the Eid. Tasty snacks are given to visitors. The pastry triangles below are filled with spinach and pine nuts.

watching for the new moon. When they spot it, the *Eid* can begin.

Early the next day everybody gets up and dresses in their best clothes. In the small villages some of the girls and even the women paint special, traditional patterns on their hands with a red-brown dye.

After a tasty breakfast people hurry to the mosque to give thanks to God, while at home women prepare a midday feast for the whole family, including very distant relatives. When visitors arrive, they call out *"Eid Mubarak!"* which means "Happy

Muslim greetings cards are very pretty, but they never show pictures of people or animals. Muslims believe only God can create living creatures, so people should not try to copy Him.

festival!" All children receive gifts of money, and the girls get pretty pieces of jewelry.

The following day friends and neighbors visit, and this continues until everyone is tired and the children have spent all their gift money on toys, candy, or fun fair rides.

Eid Al-Fitr happens 10 to 12 days earlier each year because it is timed on the sighting of the moon and not on the Western calendar.

DRIED FRUIT SALAD

SERVES FOUR
2 cups dried apricots
1 cup dried prunes
½ cup raisins
½ cup blanched almonds
1 T. pine nuts
1 T. pistachios, shelled
1 cup of water
2 T. orange juice

Put all the ingredients except the orange juice into a pan and stir together. Cook over a low heat for 25 minutes.

Remove eight of the apricots and purée them in the blender with the orange juice and some of the cooking liquid. Stir the purée into the fruit mixture to thicken the sauce. Chill and serve cold.

MAKE A RAMADAN DRUMMER

These drummers are usually cut from metal. In Lebanon they hang in the entrances of restaurants during Ramadan.

For centuries Lebanon was part of the Turkish Ottoman Empire. The Turkish rulers were Muslim, and the Turkish court was very grand. During Ramadan in the old days of the empire drums would roll at sunset to announce the end of the day's fast. This little figure is a reminder of those times.

YOU WILL NEED
Cardboard
Craft paint
Scissors
Thread
Metal paper fastener

1 Draw drummer and arm onto cardboard. Cut out.

2 Mark position, then pierce hole in armless shoulder of drummer.

3 Mark position, then pierce hole into top of arm. Mark position, then pierce hole into bend of arm. Paint arm and figure. Allow to dry. At top of arm tie long thread through hole and around edge of cardboard. Knot securely.

4 To make a tassel, wind thread several times around small square of cardboard. Carefully pull wound thread off cardboard. Hold wound thread in center and, using thread attached to arm, tie it close to one end of wound thread. Snip through loops of wound thread at untied end.

5 Line up hole at mid-arm and hole on shoulder. Secure together with paper fastener. Pull the tassel to make drummer bang his drum!

21

EID AL-ADHA

About ten weeks after Ramadan has ended, Muslim families prepare for the "Festival of the Sacrifice." This is a major festival to recall the prophet Abraham's devotion to God.

This *Eid* happens on the tenth day of the twelfth month of the Muslim calendar. It comes after the *Hajj* – a pilgrimage that millions of devout Muslims make each year to Mecca, where Mohammed was born.

The origin of this festival lies in a story told in both the Bible and the Koran. A long time ago the prophet Abraham was ready to make a sacrifice of his own son. However, God told him to kill a lamb instead.

Many families buy a sheep or a lamb some time before the festival. The animal is fattened up on mulberry and vine leaves. In towns sheep can be seen living on the balconies of apartment houses!

Just before the festival a butcher is called to slaughter the animal according to religious rules. The butcher says a short prayer, *"Allah Akbar"* – "God is great," three times before he cuts the sheep's throat.

The big day begins early, and everybody wears their best, or even new, clothes and goes to pray at the mosque. The whole lamb is served at midday, stuffed with rice, pine nuts, almonds, and ground meat in a recipe called *kharouf mehshi*. All the relatives turn up and give gifts

Many pilgrims bring home pieces of amber and semiprecious stones from Mecca. These can be made into jewelry, as gifts for friends.

to the children. Then friends visit, or the family goes visiting. Wealthy people must give some of the food to the poor so that everybody can enjoy *Eid Al-Adha*.

If anybody has made the pilgrimage to Mecca that year, their home will be decorated in green bunting and with painted or stitched quotes from the Koran. Pilgrims all bring back gifts, such as dates, amber, semiprecious stones, and *z a m - z a m* water. This water is said to have powers to heal and soothe the faithful.

THE LAMB OF LUCK

When a family is having a lot of bad luck, they buy a festive lamb and, instead of eating it, they give all the meat away in the hope that this will please God.

None of the lamb is wasted. The brains are a delicacy and so is the liver, served raw with onions or barbecued on a skewer. Tender meat is pounded and mixed with cracked wheat and herbs to make *kibbeh*, the national dish. Fatty parts are melted for lard. The stomach is cooked with rice and nuts.

A great deal of coffee is drunk. It may be served on its own, but on a festive day it will come with fruit, chocolates, or candy such as this baklava.

THE LIFE OF MOHAMMED

During Ramadan Muslim children everywhere are taught about Mohammed. He was a shepherd boy who grew up to become God's messenger. He spread the lessons that the other prophets and Jesus brought to the world.

MOHAMMED was born more than 1,400 years ago in the desert city of Mecca, in what is now called Saudi Arabia. His mother and father died when he was very young, and he was brought up by his uncle Abu Bakr.

Mohammed spent his boyhood as a shepherd watching over sheep in the desert. When he was a young man, he looked after camels and went on long journeys to trade goods. He quickly gained a reputation as being a very honest young man.

One day a rich widow named Khadijah heard about him and went to see him. They fell in love and were married when he was 25 years old.

Mohammed was very good at calming people and settling arguments among the desert tribes, but he was very upset by their violence. He began to spend time alone in the desert, thinking about good and evil.

One day in the year 611 he was alone, sitting in a desert cave when he saw a vision of the archangel Gabriel and heard a voice saying, "Recite! Recite!" This frightened him at first, but he slowly he understood that the voice was giving him an order from

Allah. He also realized Gabriel was giving him, Mohammed, the wisdom of Allah with lessons on how a good person should behave.

Mohammed began to preach to the desert tribes that there was only one Allah and that everyone was equal, no matter who they were. This angered the rich merchants who made money from the pagan idols at Mecca – the stone statues some people worshipped. But, others followed his teachings, and they were very glad to see these statues destroyed. They wanted everyone to to follow Mohammed and, in his honor, they made Mecca a place of worship.

Like most people at that time, Mohammed did not read or write, but he "recited" the angel's messages to scholars, who carefully wrote them down. These writings were gathered together to form the Koran, the Muslim holy book.

ASHURA

This festive day celebrates three events. It is a very important time for Muslims, who hold all members of Mohammed's family in deep respect.

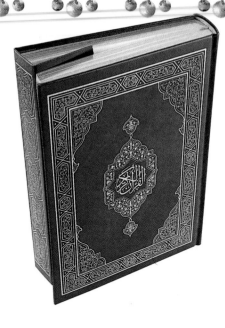

According to a Muslim belief, it was on this day that Noah and his Ark reached dry land after the Flood, and Moses led the Israelites out of Egypt, where they had been slaves. It also commemorates the death of Hussein, Mohammed's grandson, and Hussein's family and friends.

Most people in Lebanon are Shi'ah Muslims, and this is an especially important festival for this sect. Their differences with other Muslims stem from ancient loyalty to the family of Hussein.

For many days before *Ashura* mothers tell their children the story of Hussein and his people, who were trapped in the desert by soldiers sent by an evil man named Yazid.

The story tells how Hussein begged all his people to leave him and save themselves,

Children are read lessons from the holy book, the Koran. These books are honored, and cared for, by Muslim families. The pages below are from a beautifully decorated version.

but nobody obeyed him. Hussein and his people were killed one by one. Each man and each boy died with a sword in one hand and the holy Koran in the other. Last to die was brave Hussein, pierced by 33 lance and sword thrusts.

Though it all happened 1,300 years ago, these stories still make people sad and some even weep. Afterward they drink tea, and the children are given *raha* candies called Turkish delight.

On the day of Ashura men and boys form processions and act out the sad story of Hussein. Some even hit themselves to make-believe they are suffering like Hussein did. The procession ends with a play. In it the angel Gabriel

has a great key that can open the gates of Paradise to those who honor Hussein.

At the feast many people bring with them ingredients to make a mutton broth called *hireeseh*. It is stirred all night in huge pots in the courtyard of the mosque. The broth is shared with the needy.

This is a good-luck charm to hang on a wall. Muslims believe that this symbol of a hand and horseshoe will help protect them from bad luck.

Crossed swords like these are favorite wall decorations in Lebanon. They recall the bravery of Mohammed's grandson, Hussein, and Hussein's loyal followers.

27

EID IL MILAD

Lebanese Christians celebrate Christmas as the "Festival of the Birth." December is cold here, so Christmas is celebrated indoors with much good food.

Going to church on Christmas Eve is a happy, noisy family occasion. People let off fireworks and shoot rifles into the air as the churchbells ring. The bells are very heavy, and young men in the villages try to impress the girls in a competition to see who can pull hardest on the bell ropes.

A long time ago Arab Christians, such as the Maronites, did not celebrate the birth of Jesus on December 25 as do most other Christians. Maronite families gave presents at New Year instead of Christmas.

Nowadays most homes are decorated with fir trees covered in Christmas lights. Placed near the tree so

The pretty and sturdy flat cushions below are called tarraahat. *People sit on them near the fire while playing games, listening to stories, or nibbling from a bowl of nuts.*

that everyone can see it will be a nativity, a model scene showing the birth of Jesus in a manger.

Father Christmas also brings gifts for the children on Christmas Eve when they are asleep. On Christmas Day custom lets the children beg for more gifts by shouting out *"Editi 'aleik"* – "You have a gift for me!" – at every adult they meet!

The Christmas turkey or chicken is yet another tradition that is familiar in the West. However, in Lebanon many women prefer to buy their birds live. They buy them long before the festive day so they can fatten the birds up and be certain that the meat on the table is as fresh as can be.

During November turkey sellers are a

This old image of Baby Jesus and His mother comes from a holy book used at the Maronite Mass. It is written in Arabic and Syriac, a language from the time of Jesus.

common sight, as they shepherd their large flocks of turkeys along the village streets.

Everyone in Lebanon enjoys sweet foods and candy, especially at this time of the year. Special favorites include *baklava* pastries and *knafi*, layers of cheese in a baked, shredded wheat, covered with a sweet syrup.

There is plenty of sugared candy, nougat, figs, oranges, apples, raisins, figs, walnuts, and bowls of mixed seeds and small nuts to nibble on.

Muslims are not allowed alcohol, but Lebanese Christians celebrate Christmas with a grape drink called Araq.

FAMILY GAMES

There are all sorts of games to play on cold winter's nights. *Basra* is a party-time favorite. It is a guessing-game like charades. *Chadeh* are card games. They include *pinochle*, canasta, and bridge for the adults. *Dama* is a kind of checkers, and there is dominoes and chess. Backgammon has been played in Lebanon for thousands of years. Most families have a backgammon board, often beautifully hand-made.

EID ISSAYYDI

This Christian feast takes place at the height of summer. It is a happy celebration to mark the day the Virgin Mary was received into Heaven.

Eid *Issayydi* means the "Festival of Our Lady." It is also called Virgin Mary Day and Assumption Day. This happy festival takes place on August 15. It begins, however, the night before, when wood fires are lit under giant cooking pots filled with sheep bones, mutton, and raw wheat. Excited crowds stay up late to watch the bubbling brew being stirred until it becomes a thick broth. This *hireeseh* is also made by Muslims when they celebrate *Ashura*. The churches are filled with summer flowers for morning Mass, and afterward everyone eats the hireeseh.

WORDS TO KNOW

Fast: To go without some or all kinds of food and drink deliberately.

Koran: The Islamic holy book, believed to be the word of God as told to the prophet Mohammed.

Maronites: A Christian sect living mainly in Lebanon. The Maronites are recognized by the pope as a branch of the Roman Catholic Church.

Mass: A Christian ritual in which bread and wine are used to commemorate the Last Supper of Jesus Christ.

Mecca: The birthplace of Mohammed. Mecca is the most important place of pilgrimage for Muslims.

Mosque: A place of worship for Muslims.

Patron saint: A saint who is special to a particular group. Nations, towns, and professions have patron saints.

Phoenician: Citizen of Phoenicia, a nation that thrived in the pre-Christian era.

Pilgrim: A person who makes a religious journey, or pilgrimage, to a holy place.

Prophet: A teacher or interpreter of the will of God.

Ramadan: The ninth month of the Muslim year, during which Muslims fast from dawn until sunset.

Resurrection: The rising of Christ from the dead on Easter Sunday.

Roman Catholic: A member of the Roman Catholic Church, the largest branch of Christianity. The head of this church is the pope.

Sacrifice: To give up something that is greatly valued for an even more important reason.

Sect: A group whose religious beliefs differ from those of others who practice the same religion.

Shi'ahs: A group of Muslims who believe that the descendants of Mohammed's grandson, Hussein, are his rightful successors.

Sunnis: A group of Muslims who believe that the four elected rulers of Islam are Mohammed's rightful successors.

ACKNOWLEDGMENTS

WITH THANKS TO:
L'Artisans du Liban. Panache, London. Father Paul Melhem, Maronite Mission, London. A. Jarrah, Director, Lebanon Tourist Office, London.

PHOTOGRAPHY:
All photographs by Bruce Mackie except: John Elliott pp. 13, 19. Marshall Cavendish pp. 12, 18, 23. Cover photograph by Corbis/Owen Franken.

ILLUSTRATIONS BY:
Fiona Saunders pp. 4 – 5. Tracy Rich p. 7.
Maps by John Woolford.

Recipes: Ellen Dupont.

Set Contents